Graffiti in the City

Ridhima Bhagawati

BookLeaf Publishing
India | USA | UK

Made with ❤ on the BookLeaf Publishing Platform
www.bookleafpub.in
www.bookleafpub.com

*To Mamma, Pappa, and Rimli Baa: my earliest
muses.*

Acknowledgements

Now, where on earth to begin?

Writing poems is supposed to be a solitary endeavor, yet I couldn't feel more supported and encouraged than I do now. All the savvy consultants, agents, designers, and editors at BookLeaf Publishing helped me mass-produce my ideas and put together my scribbled notes into the book in your hands. Thank you to Farida Khan, my publishing consultant who guided me every step of the way (including answering my 3 a.m. questions), and to Mujtaba Feroz Shah, for his picture-perfect cover designs that breathed life into the immaterial. Thank you to my draft editor Ritika, for polishing my draft and making it worthy of printing. Although I couldn't meet or get acquainted with them by name, their passion for poems and wordplay has inspired countless poets, including me. This book wouldn't exist without the blood and sweat of those savvy employees staying up making those tutorials, hand-holding us through the entire process and answering every stupid question we may have. Trust me, no one knows what it's like to get late-night emails like these guys. Their professionalism and expertise helped turn my muddled ideas into something tangible. They made this book as much as I did.

Speaking of those who helped craft this book, a shout-out to my incredible muses. This book features a lot of characters that I plucked straight from my school and neighborhood. I tried to listen to good-old Ruskin Bond when he said that one doesn't need to look beyond their immediate vicinity for inspiration. To my beloved girls gang: Kiara, Elina, Myra, Archisha, Ishika, and Shivanshi, for bringing more than enough "crazy" into my life and pulling me out of the house whenever I needed it. To my maverick schoolmates, Ira, Levitha, Viresh, Ahaan, Inaya, Arayna, Rose, Vaidehi, Vedant, Abhiraj, Aarna, Dhruv, Sakhi, Tisha, Vivaan, and Himaank, for filling my brain to the brim with stories and anecdotes that helped bring this book to life (To my oblivious muses, look closely, I'm sure you guys can find yourselves written somewhere into these pages). This book belongs to all of you as much as it does to me.

And if we're talking about muses, I can't leave out Taylor Swift, Ruelle, Olivia Rodrigo, Tyler Hoechlin's 'Superman and Lois', Grant Gustin's 'The Flash', Stephen Amell's 'Green Arrow', Jane Austen, Marissa Meyer's incredible series *Lunar Chronicles*, or Shreya Ghoshal for igniting my mind and soul to just the right temperature for poetry.

The biggest thank you in the whole world to my three lifelines—Mamma, Pappa, and Rimli Baa (That's Assamese for 'older sister'). Mamma, for being my spine, clearing away everything in my path that could lead me astray and for always being the first person to experience my poems. Pappa, for taking a disproportionately large amount of pride in the words I write and in the person he and my mamma have raised me to be. Thank you

Pappa, for buying me hundreds of books in the blink of an eye, pushing me to stoke the fires of my literary interests, cultivating my passion for language all my life and for being my favorite person to talk to when it comes to literature. Lastly, thank you to my college-going older sister Rishika, for being the partner-in-crime that every teenage girl needs. It's because of her I learned how to write my ABCs, how to add and subtract, how to pick out good shows from the litter, and how to let my heart be inspired by art. Thanks to her I fell in love with music, poetry, books, stories, and writing.

Thank you to my grandparents, my drop-dead gorgeous aunts, my uncles, and my wild cousins—for being a home away from home, and to every other person on this planet who became a poem for me. Our house-help Miss Swati and her adorable 4-year-old Mao, the staff and teachers at my school, the beloved English teacher Miss Jasmine for teaching me how much literature and words can mean to a person and how much school has to offer. The lady at the tiny lace store in Clover Centre with impeccable taste in fashion, and Dr. Susan Thomas and Sir Precious Pherim for being my number-one fans since day one and bringing the fun in literature at every turn. Thank you to my neighbors, Rajesh Uncle and Manjusha Auntie, to my friends, to my comrades, and to everyone who's lit me up with inspiration by merely existing the way they are. Thank you, thank you, thank you, to all of you.

And finally, thank you so, so, so much to you, dear reader, the one holding this book in your hands. You are the one to claim my words for your own the moment your eyes fall on them. You are the ones to feel the emotions embedded in each rhyme and meter. You are the ones who, just like me, fit neatly and imperfectly—in a poem.

Preface

Ted Kooser once said, "There are mornings when everything brims with promise, even my empty cup."

There is a new Gen-Z trend circulating online, centered around the idea of "romanticizing your life." It sounds really simple: wake up feeling like a Disney princess in a canopy bed, feigning perfection and faking happiness. Being eccentric, observant, hopeful—in today's fast-tracked world, these are all "trends". Saying anything personal or "deep" feels overtly maverick nowadays. And me? I'm just like other girls. I'm up-to-date and well-acquainted. For the past 14 years of my life I have been meticulously crafting the perfect social-security insurance plan. And that isn't just true for me. 60% of us have forgotten who we are while competing in this rat race. But deep down, we all hope that our lives truly *can* be like those coming-of-age movies: revelational and epic. . . That is when

I realized what "romanticizing your life" really means. That is when I understood what Ted Kooser was actually talking about. An empty coffee cup *does* hold promise. So does the Pune City skyline, as well as handmade cards, pickles, chocolate, emails, and musicals.

The poets pride themselves on discovering their eccentricities by "dressing their thoughts in the form of a poem," as Elizabeth Acevedo puts it. I grew up reading quotes and anecdotes of people who seemed to preserve snippets of their lives on paper. Hundreds of poets, hundreds of perspectives on the same-old human problems. I remember finding a Ruskin Bond book titled *How to Be a Writer* at the airport. I remember it saying: "There are so many lovely things to see, there is so much to do, so much fun to be had and so many charming and interesting people to meet. How can my pen ever run dry?"

That, right there, is why I've written this book. There are too many songs stuck in my head, too many verses dancing and rolling on my tongue; too many dishes with a lingering smell, too many cafés and memories. Too many wonderful people, too many effervescent places, too many joys and too many frustrations, too many things that vex me and exasperate me. The hunt for another kindred spirit is never-ending. The best way to put it is in Major Gilbert's quote from *Violet Evergarden*: "To let her heart be inspired by beauty...I wanted that for her."

So to let our hearts be inspired, forward we go, into slam poetry on paper: *Graffiti in the City*.

The Hook

"What is the genre of your life?"

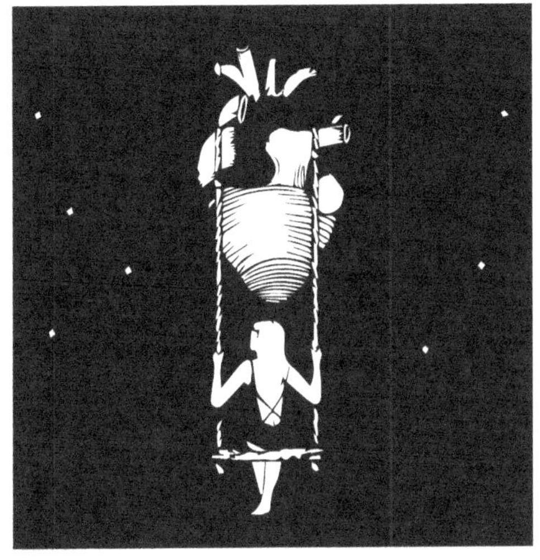

She asked me, square-eyed

Like iron, her face magnetized

Her calves beaten raw by the waves

Grasping my collar, by the wind swayed.

I answer, "It was a thriller, action-packed and swift,

Tantalizing death as I rode off the cliffs."

My main character, then, asked me, "And now?"

"Now it's a coming-of-age, darling," I vowed.

You Want to Know Who I Am?

My favorite words are *wistful* and *love*

So I know I was made

to have my heart broken.

My favorite sound is of the violin's undertones

So I know I am

a poem unspoken.

You'll find me in every "sorry"

you have, in your life, ever heard.

For it seems like "Sorry for being awful"

are becoming my second-favorite words.

But if you grab a chart paper,

and cut up some words to make a collage,

you'll find me somewhere in the mess of
syllables,

playing semantic espionage.

Now tell me, where can I find you?

Narcissist

I am a Narcissist,

because my best dress,

is living wild.

For I know I look,

stunning when,

I look utterly alive.

Life's Message

Life came down in the rain

and love stirred in the empty street

the moment was perfect, as both

feelings mixed like soup

and warmed me up inside

that I opened my arms

and I shut my eyes

and surrendered.

Moon River

"Moon River," she sang,

leaning, breathing, into the mic;

as she grabbed ahold of her bare chest;

as the indoor holy energies spiked.

And the higher she sang, the higher she rose,

mouth contorting in glee;

as she doused the air and dipped her heart

in glitter so all could see.

Such Mornings

Such mornings that resonate,

like music, to your bed from the sun;

such hours that illuminate,

and light the face of how far you've come.

Such mornings when you wake,

with the kiss of dew all over you,

Such hours, when golden-clad you rise,

and there's not a piece missing out of you.

A pleasantness, embracing every part of you.

The Protagonists

Newborn Baby

On a pearly face of milky white,

the blush of blood squeezed through.

And in eyes a sticky, slimy brown,

the rush of creation lightly cooed.

Like candy unwrapped from crinkly paper,

her senses slowly unfurled to youth.

As she smelled all; but the smell in our nose,

was of the candy-baby's sweetening tooth.

Lights don't lie

You tell me,

You are the shadows

But I see you when your heart

Is breaking

And I see the moon reflecting off

The tear in your eye

And the glistening sweat of a nightmare

In your waking.

Genius

The way his jaw fell,

as he saw them humans in action,

the way his rolling eyes could tell,

that he was brewing concoctions.

The way we know he knows,

that we know he's an evil genius.

The way his putrid ego shows

bordering on something heinous.

The Musician

You know when his physique,

Dissolves in sensation

And his eyes glint,

In manifestation;

That he has sold his soul,

To the devil in exchange,

And there is no saving him,

From his dead-man's stage.

The leading lady

From a titanium throat, she spat wisdom

Gesturing to the moon

And roused the unlit acres of faces

One sunny afternoon.

The pendulum struck with her bobbing head

Her bare feet sank in the mud

The paint of the tricolor dripped from her chest

A striking silhouette in the sun.

Performer

Waving maniacally, from the zenith of the stage

Inviting the masses on viral tape

Pinned on a trophy, she fled her cage

As she spun for the audience in a fit of rage.

Her eyes widened as the curtains rose

Oozing years of modelling, she struck a pose

And just like that the girl was flattened

From audience-fed therapy, the performer
was maddened.

The Man

The nuances of his sugar gaze,

Enraptured ladies in a deodorant haze;

His large tongue, the tip on fire,

Always in larger-than-life attire.

And his delicately woven speech,

Perfection that lies far out of reach;

For laymen, cavemen, and dreamy boys,

With eyes of oak and muscle alloy.

He is beautiful, invulnerable,

Undefeated and so honorable;

One look from him can massacre a village,

He, the good god, and the exquisite image.

Girl's Girl

Ladies, livid lionesses!

spill bills out of your purse.

Flip your braided hair, your highness,

and lift the golden hem of your skirt.

And the voice that whispered, timid and sweet,

now giggle, scream, throat ablaze.

The eyes that fixated downcast, meek,

now blink like a petty flirt in a daze.

Those hands adorned with golden strings,

and bodices shining like skies on their chest.

In this night-museum of pretty things,

these girls, they sparkle colors over the rest.

The gusto, the zest, the laugh, the sarcasm,

in her voice as she sings those songs.

Cutting through the room in a light-filled
spasm,

parading through the gawking throngs.

The auction is set, but no one dares,

to try their luck tonight.

For the beacon in the room, collecting stares,

are the girls in their skirts who own the night.

The Family

Life and Stories

My mother is exactly what

Stories should be like—

That come to you, oblivious,

And leave you, newly wise.

My mother is exactly what

Life and stories should be like—

That are given to you, to love and cherish,

And can save you utterly before you perish.

Long Lost Lovers

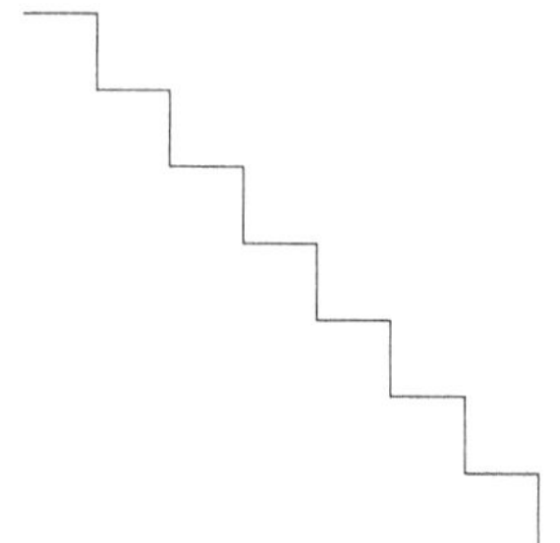

I pattered down the stairs,

like rain battered down the hill.

My calves burned with sweat,

like the screaming that shrouded and
crowded my head.

For your footsteps, opposite me, ran up,

as if with rosy dawn the angels were waking
up.

Our gazes clashed and shuddered,

like the winds, striking, and tentative, hover.

The words, insipid, yet choking my throat,

like with rushing water the river broke.

I looked quickly away, picking the shards,

those scattered pieces of rose-colored glass.

For when we saw each other on those stairs,

like crossing vehicles, we nodded and passed.

As if neither of us had anything to say;

as if neither of us had heavy hearts.

Inadequate Vocabulary

I prefer to hug,

And kiss her than

To tell her by mouth,

How I feel truly.

For I know if I tried,

To find the words I do not know,

It would all come out,

Inadequate and unruly.

Syllabus

Mothers have so much to say,

And so much to teach,

Yet very few days.

So tell me, mother,

All of it, in one piece.

Or I might just never,

Leave you in peace.

Happy Accidents

When my sister

Opened my journal

She read the secrets

I could never show her

myself.

It's like she found

The heart that I wait

For someone to pick up and read;

Which I could never offer

myself.

Her little deeds

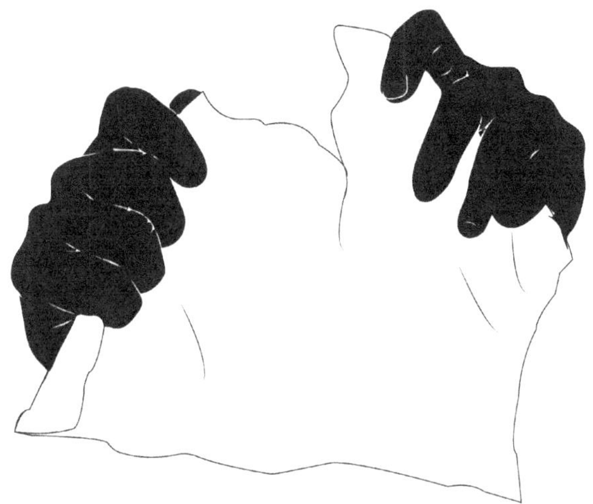

I watched her weave stories

As she worked the cloth in her hands,

Brows furrowed in focus,

Fingers telling a tale,

For many years.

That if all the world could hear,

They would rise from their seats,

In tears.

Your baby

Chasing, chasing till I drop dead

Just when will it be enough?

How big, how tall, how giant I dream.

How distant, how cold, how lost I become

How simple it is to be your baby

When it is okay to be small

I can curl up and sleep, small and weak,

And I needn't change myself at all.

My Mother Says

My mother said that all of us,

create our own world.

Shard by shard we build our dome,

and try to mold our play-dough globe.

My mother said that all of me,

resides in said abode.

And my Earth has the sweetest fruits,

and daffodils with growing shoots.

But most of all, my mother says,

that when she sees my Earth;

she says that every springing stride,

through my lawns, fills her with pride.

THE ARTIST

Holi

I promise to stain your colorless shirt,

to paint you pink and yellow.

I promise to stuff you in a sack,

and drag you, save you, from your sorrow.

I promise to vandalize your soul,

and render life your smash toy.

I promise to teach you happiness,

so take my colored hand, boy.

Liar

The most beautiful girl in the world,

mahogany-brown skin and eyes;

a body shaped of cedar wood,

smelling sweet, the scent of lies.

You, my friend, have healed me plenty,

before you pulled my skin open wide;

you have grown daisies on my grave,

but also been the one to wake me to life.

For in your sweet heart-shaped eyes,

I have seen hellfire's rising tide;

but in my heart, I've seen you more,

to know, by heart, what you're like inside.

So let the cement peel away,

and let those hateful tears fly;

for once, let me hear you scream,

let me see what you are dying to hide.

Graffiti in the city

The acrylic life of those long dead,

are dreams etched in graffiti art.

Bodies, minds, frozen in time;

colorful fossils of the heart.

Those sneakers, fakers, traversing through,

the dark, shrouded city streets,

are haunted by the revolution;

an inanimate voice that loudly speaks.

Thunder

Pages, flip wildly,

Ink, fly lively,

Lift my soul like an offering

Drop me, free-falling, from the buildings

And rush me, speedy, accelerating so far,

That the wind whips my measly sleeves apart

That the skies all blend in a shooting-starred
blur

And everybody marvels at my bolt of
thunder.

Christmas Painting

Wildflower gown, splattering colors

in a stormy roundabout of paint,

a skirt with wings and a tongue catching rain.

Fire-red hair, flinging embers,

scorching frost off the heart,

kinetic energy to light a spark.

And a white, crystalline December

casting white spots on golden-brown skin,

wearing net-stockings thin.

Dancer's Monument

The talk of the dancer's monument,

is nothing short of strange.

That spectacle, it shook the world,

and championed for change.

They say the builders had tiny builds,

and hearts soft as clay.

Not one brought a single brick,

or wrench that fateful day.

They were empty-handed, grains of sand,

with only shoes to dance.

One jump, and a foundation was lain,

and then the show began.

The girls, their hair, their heels, their skirts;

the boys, their passion galore,

grew pillars, like shoots, an arched roof,

and diamond-clad floors.

It was coined the "Dancer's monument,"

and it was only the first to come.

For the parade, the revolution born,

would shake the whole world numb.

THE NIGHT-BANDIT

Devil's Love Story

I wrote a hundred letters to the angels

But the devil's footsoldiers read the labels

So I received gift packages carrying light

As the angels were credited by the very dark
knight.

I fell in love with a honeydew smile

Which turned out to be a facsimile

As the enchanting man winked to the one
behind me

And followed his instructions to pacify me.

Yet I never stopped looking, my curiosity a thorn

In the devil's side, in his tailored lore

Ignoring his protests, I peeled the charcoal

To reveal veins with too much blood to gargle.

"Not so evil after all," I grinned,

Mirroring his rehearsed expression of sin

"You may fool them, but dare you fool me?"

Then his eyes softened, as I set him free.

Loose-Tongued

Our meeting was tongue-tied, old,

our journey was loose-tongues, gold.

Our parting was heavy-tongues, raw,

smiling through a heart-broken jaw.

Our togetherness was smiles,

our separation stretched for miles,

yet our tongues came loose, free,

every time we embraced each other in glee.

Honest Retina

On each colorful eye's retina,

Lies the most dishonest mirror of all.

How many doppelgangers I have seen,

In them, I can't recall.

I am blind to every one of my clones,

In the rest of the world's eyes.

Except one, that every science approves of,

that no other retina can defy

I am a slave to whatever I see,

Or think I do in your mirror,

So please, look at me with the same retina

through every altering decade that goes by my mother.

I don't mind shape-shifting,

Into whatever you see of me.

But keep in mind I will move heaven and Earth,

To erase every disappointment that you see.

Stadium Lights

Stadium lights glaring in the night,

we tumbled into the world.

Pure energy, pure madness,

drinking in the salt of the Earth.

"At the stroke of the midnight hour,"

the legend, the veteran smiled over.

As we were released, too much for the
airplanes to carry,

philistines cowering in the corner.

Hotel Vacation

Long-cracked feet now sparkle,

moist coolness slipping between our toes,

long-stretched muscles now loosened,
breathe,

relaxed and dormant.

The sweet ache of lingering back pain,

which only flares like a healing heat,

as I lay against my pillow, in a quilt,

warm as chocolate, lost in a dream.

When I Was Young

Have you ever heard of psychometry?

The power to see the urban past?

To peer into the souls of folktales old,

and read the inscriptions that last.

For in the stone-age cave of my youth,

I found pristine time capsules due.

In the coma of growth, I flashbacked before,

to revisit manuscripts of forgotten lore.

Now to excavate the monument,

I went to that ancient café;

equipped with wisdom and resurfaced
memories,

and the lingering smell of an age-old latte.

My mother, with memory clear as glass,

told me about our golden past.

The memories of a café scattered in pieces,

like clear handwriting on a paper with
creases.

"There used to be a carnival below.

And the owners knew us well by name.

These marble tables were wooden stools.

The white-washed walls had coffee stains."

The pasta tasted like something I'd lost,

like a bundle of treasures melted out of frost.

So here I am, remembering anew,

in different clothes, eating the same menu.

Princess-Gown

I sat like a portrait, frozen in paint,

every joint a work of art and grace,

as the bodice pulled my back up straight,

and transformed me into a royal portrait.

My Shadow

Worry not, I have no secrets

And never will till the day I die,

For there is a witness to my every sin

To whom I simply cannot lie.

Her green eyes haunt me everywhere

Like a phantom, her gaze lingers close

In my head, beneath my bed,

The empty seat, the neighbouring street

They were there when I lied to my friends

They were there when I lied to myself

They have always been within the walls,

Beside me, under the stars.

They were there in the room, those sleepless
nights,

They watched me as I slowly died

Unknowingly, unintentionally,

They were the shadows by my side.

They stalked me everywhere I went

Testing me, guiding me,

Reminding me of a beautiful past

and parts of me that had already passed.

They existed—I just know they did,

A window in the soundproof room,

They stood, unwavering, unforgiving,

between myself and my doom.

Too Late

Long ago, I stepped up,

to your yard to wait.

I brushed my boots, laden with soot

to fix my battered state.

Leaves fell and regrew, anew,

as excitement started to wane.

And the warmth of the past that carried me
hither

morphed into pain.

Eons passed, till you arrived,

and found me on the steps.

You embraced my wrinkled face in tears,

until the decay set.

Star-Crossed

Grains of rice, dots of people,

accumulating there.

Stretching the world, the plate, the sky,

retreating to a common lair.

For the color of your heart tells me more,

than your name ever could.

So your hand in mine is destiny,

saying everything that poems should.

Tortured Artist

Peach arms and blue eyes,

leapt off of the page.

A graphite border, thick and deep,

flew in a nasty fit of rage.

For every time a passerby,

looked to the canvas for hope,

Black Dahlias doused in paint,

shook as the artist's heart broke.

Autobiography

Yelling boy, tearing his throat

Surrounded by people, who seem to care but
don't

His tears falling back into his mouth

Vertigo spinning his mindscape south.

If he wrote an autobiography

He would fill the bibliography

With beautiful people and their souls

In a book of genres far too morose.

Nonchalance

He seethed because his lifeless eyes,

are not enough to scare;

and his nonchalance convinces none

that he does not care.

He pounds his head, for his cold pretence,

is too much for him to bear.

"If you're trying to shield me," his heart
whispered,

"Then why am I starting to tear?"

Bestie

Yes, I smile in the sun

And I turn around

To bury my face

In shadow.

Much like I smile at you

And turn around

To bury my heart

In vain.

Villain's Arc

Stones, the shape of winged eyes,

stabbing, stabbing, bloody Sunday.

Whispering sharp to chip your mind,

and scatter the pieces far away.

The points, they graze at your skin,

scratching, bloodshed, wreaking carnage.

Until the daggers rise from your heart

to testify that you have been tarnished.

Torture-Training

I trained myself

to remain untouchable

unaffected, unfazed

and when my shelter of foliage tumbled over,

the rain tore me apart—

untrained.

DAWN

Lifeline

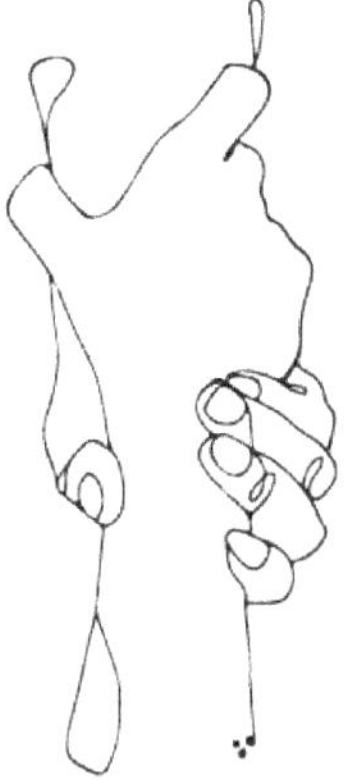

My want for life,

Will always waver.

Unwavering are,

the hands that will hold onto me,

against my kicking and thrashing:

the hands that will not let me leave.

Midnight Dawn

The glorious unveiling of daybreak, dawn,

poured into the bedroom in the middle of the night;

as a lifeless shell of a child widened his eyes,

his small face turning to the light.

In a buried basement, orchestras rose,

a shadowed town, a shadowed home;

and like a revelation, the light bulbs glowed,

passions burning as Christmas snowed,

Hearts racing as time slowed.

Moon Audience

To the boy,

who stands on the chilling threshold,

of the windowsill, staring at the moon;

who traces

the tiles of his bedroom floor

every lonely afternoon.

To the girl who clutches

her wine-dark locks,

and tear-stains the mirror;

to the child

playing dress-up, screaming into a pillow,

eroding his youth, a sacrificial giver.

To the teenager

hiding behind her clothes,

wishing she could crush or swap her bones;

to the toddler

pulling sleeves to his wrist,

his pale, chubby arms so prematurely toned.

To the warrior

who smiles and cries

with regret for pampering her soul;

to the kid

who's sleepy but has no bed,

who's been told, too often, "You're on your own."

Every poet, painter, and lily-pad angel,

draws her miracle-magic from you.

Cracking diamonds out of sandstone shells,

shining through and through.

I heard a saying, that when you look

at the moon, somewhere, there's always
another;

my darling, broken, lonely moon audience:

Look around! For there are many others.

The World Is Yours

When every inch of the earthly sky

bores holes into you,

and the silence of blue midnight

rings orchestral and true.

When the edges of your humdrum being

itch with solitude,

and the deepest cavities in your heart,

illuminate through and through.

Such nights when the mind

paints you a paradise,

and a premonition dawns

on you to revolutionize.

The universe expands itself

like childbirth before your eyes,

and the world lays itself at your feet

daring you to fantasize.

Meteors

I called a big audience,

of all the people who ever spoke my name,

and in one swift motion, I unraveled like a ribbon,

and stretched across the entire stage.

Pieces of me flew like meteors,

crashing between the many chairs,

scaring away almost everyone,

Except you, who stayed right there.

Superman and Lois

The Man of Steel; he touched the sun;

the star-shaped silhouette, the hero.

He carried embers and emblems strong;

he ignited hearts and citizens along.

And behind him, unrelenting, she stood,

smiling, singing, his name on her chest.

Like his star, she drew him his Krypton sky,

and gave him a lap to rest his head.

And by they came, those beastly boys;

like fire and ice, rabid and wild.

To wear his heart on their body, the
super-youth;

the sons of the Earth, the champions of truth.

By came the fires, by came the quake,

leaving a deathly smell in its wake;

crumbling hearts, he fell to his knees.

His tears grew waves that dissolved in the sea.

The rocks and knives that left him scathed;

her hand, it wiped the tears on his face.

The boys, they dreamed like no night before,

and lifted him mighty, forevermore.

Their kisses, they stamped onto his heart;

their breaths, they pushed him on his back.

Their hands, they grasped for a hand to hold,

their cries, they begged for him to come back.

The Man of Steel; he touched the Earth,

the broken angel, the wounded man.

Leaning against her shoulder, his hand on
their head,

to his girls, to his boys, he quietly said:

"You are my anthem, I'll fly away now

and come running back to you, my love.

My girl, my boys, you stay within."

For as long as they live, there's some fight left in him.

Fighters

She and her mother, brown-skinned,

walk with scars, wings singed,

arms bare without a woolen coat

in the winter, stripped of hope.

Just today, amidst the giant buildings,

I saw them on the bicycle, clutching

the rails; them mother-daughter slowly
wheeling

on their daily commute, promised a feeling.

That mother's smile, as she jokingly cried,

carrying her scars with sweaty pride,

as the girl grew under one wing alone,

chubby and sweet in a feathery home.

Her skinny frame could cover her child,

enveloping her like a diamond sky,

as it rained fire, the little girl smiles,

sweetening the tears in Mommy's eyes.

Afterlife

We know, well aware,

of the mountains that will rise,

and the plains that will expand,

before our eyes.

We know, young and wise,

of the cosmic die;

scattering us,

on either side.

And we know, heads held rightly high,

that poignantly, we shall spring to life,

and as we die, dissolve in the Earth,

to forevermore, reunite.

Sunday

Tired from laying bricks,

and checking boxes of corporate rubrics,

of burning, fanning the agita,

of sweating, climbing the rocky strata.

Body broken, the sweetness peeped,

up at me from the flower-heap,

my limping legs yawned and stretched,

dangling like a free-hand sketch.

Slow as aging, I watched the sunrise,

every golden sunray cooling my eyes.

The dew of the morning grass then began to whisper,

"Kid, how long do you intend to burn?"

Homecoming

I, the explorer, wander the world

With pomp and pomposity.

Etching the skies into my sketchbook,

Travelling for all of eternity.

And when my legs give out beneath me,

The suitcase drops out of my hand,

Before I die, I promise you,

I'll always come limping back.

We helped each other to dawn

The day a blind boy found a four-leaf clover

And dystopian empires toppled over

On a night like that with miracles true,

That was the night that I met you.

And chapters flipped, as I stood, gawked

Jaw dropping as the seasons paused

And restarted, baptismal, cleansed and
forgiven

Dragging from the shadows, bullies hidden.

And as healing people, we noticed something:

Warm and earnest, on our backs, thumping

Pushing us to dawn, as we looked down and
saw

Our hands had been joined together all along.

You did it, kid

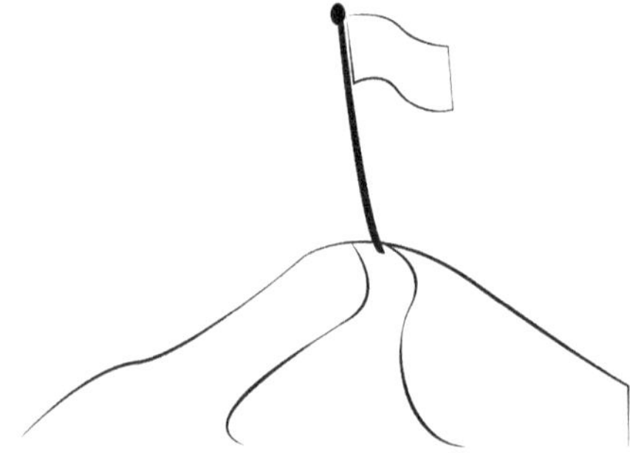

After we've put our bodies through youthful
labor,

and owed death a hundred favors,

after we've peaked and fallen in teary fervour,

and known the urge to love and murder.

After having journeyed across the seas,

to fall before paradise on your knees,

once the journey is over, all that's left to see,

are your stories in those libraries.